SWEDEN
LAND OF MANY DREAMS

Featuring the Photography of Will Curwen, Adrian Cowin & Nigel Dixon.
CLB 900/L.
© 1987 Illustrations and Text: Colour Library Books Ltd.,
   Guildford, Surrey, England.
Printed and bound in Barcelona, Spain by Cronion, S.A.
All rights reserved
1987 edition published by Crescent Books, a division of Crown Publishers, Inc.
ISBN 0.517.605155.
hgfedcba

SWEDEN
LAND OF MANY DREAMS

Text by

William Mead

Designed & Produced by
TED SMART and **DAVID GIBBON**

CRESCENT BOOKS
NEW YORK

Once upon a time there was a Swedish boy called Nils Holgersson who, since the beginning of the century, was known to all of the schoolchildren in his country. Through Nils they learned about their homeland of Sweden (*Sverige* to them) because he had the good fortune to travel the length of the country – on the back of a goose. Nils was one of the characters created by the much-loved Swedish novelist Selma Lagerlöf, and the *Wonderful Adventures of Nils*, as the tale is called, enabled him to give a bird's-eye description of the big northern land of which, in his day, rather few Swedes saw very much. True enough, the railway had already linked south Sweden's Canaan – the grain-rich province of Skane – by means of 1500 kilometres of broad-gauge track to the frosty fells of Lapland; but most Swedes were not very well-off in those days, and those who had money for travelling went in search of winter sunshine. Through Nils Holgersson's flight of fancy they became armchair travellers in their home country.

Today, Sweden is a rich country. A network of domestic air lines, filled with Swedes on their manifold business and pleasure trips, spreads some 25,000 feet above the migrating wild geese. At such an altitude, even on a clear day, cabin windows only offer a two dimensional scene – a repetitious mosaic of grey-green forests, shining water, brown rocky outcrops, oases of farmland, with towns increasingly widely spaced as you journey northwards over this long land. For Sweden is the fourth largest country in Europe, much bigger than the United Kingdom.

Sweden is situated in high latitudes. As a result, winter is the longest season, with the grey and blue of most of the countryside being transformed into the white of snow and ice for months on end. And, because winter days are short – only a few hours of daylight at midwinter in north Sweden – a flight is likely to be by night. The Swedish poet, Per Lagerqvist, wrote of "the darkness that drinks the light". It must have seemed that way to most Swedes before the coming of electricity,

which a few began to switch on about a century ago. Today, a flight by night reveals myriad pinpricks and criss-crossing ribbons of light, for now just about every Swedish home, however remote, has electricity. The stretches of utter darkness that become apparent as the aircraft flies northward to skies where the *aurora borealis* dances, impress on you the extent of the uninhabited areas.

The same northward flight in summer takes place in continuous daylight, because nearly a quarter of Sweden lies beyond the Arctic Circle and may see the midnight sun for several weeks on end. The seasonal rhythm of daylight and darkness, as well as of heat and cold, makes for striking contrasts between winter and summer in the people's work, play and attitudes.

A Dialogue between Land and Water

Descend to ground level and the repetitious landscape features as seen from the air now seem endlessly varied. Above all, it is in the interplay of land, water and woodland that Sweden's distinctive landscape lies. Off the long and intricate coastline, shared between the Baltic and the approaches to the North Sea, lie tens of thousands of islands of all shapes and sizes. In the west, the coast of the province of Bohuslän receives the full force of wind, wave and tide as they sweep in from the North Sea. Its granite islands are bald, grey, fringed with seaweed, rich in crustaceans and shellfish. Wind-trimmed vegetation matches huddled fishing villages. In the east, the approaches to Stockholm have one of the most extensive and elaborate archipelagoes in Europe. Save for its outer skerries it is wooded. It is often botanically rich, but is relatively poor in marine life. Northwards, the coast of the Gulf of Bothnia is slowly emerging from the sea. New islands and skerries, around which seals still sport, appear each century. The lakes have their own archipelagoes and, for good measure, Sweden also has two of the largest islands in the Baltic – Gotland and Öland.

Among no fewer than 90,000 lakes, Vänern, some 5,500 square kilometres in area, is the largest. It is located in the south-centre of the country, and is linked by a picturesque canal to a trio of other large lakes – Vättern, Mälaren and Hjalmaren. One of Sweden's most popular lakes is Siljan, which occupies part of a shallow limestone basin in the province of Dalarna. The northern two-thirds of Sweden rises gently from the Baltic coast through a foothill zone to mountainous heights along the Norwegian border. Here, a succession of long, narrow lakes, mostly fed by snow-melt and minor glaciers, drains by way of a series of parallel, swiftly-flowing rivers to the east. All of Sweden's rivers are characterised by waterfalls, rapids and torrents.

The dialogue between land and water also reflects the influence of rock structure and surface deposits. Most of Sweden is relatively low-lying and consists of old, hard rocks – a part of the so-called Fennoscandian Shield. The mountains folded on the western flanks of the shield were formed during a later geological period. South central Sweden, which embraces the great lakes, is much fractured and faulted. Older limestones give rise to distinctive landscapes in Gotland and Öland and, as if to show Sweden what Denmark looks like, most of the plains of the southernmost province of Skane have a bedrock of chalk. Finally, over most of the rocks is a mantle of clays of variable thickness derived from the retreating sea and the shrinking lakes, and of sandy stretches and boulder ridges which are the legacy of the Ice Age.

The Mantle of the Woodland

The natural vegetation of most of Sweden is coniferous forest – pine on the sandy and gravelly soils, spruce or Christmas trees on the moister lands, and a generous admixture of birch. Forest regeneration takes almost twice as long in the northern forests as it does in the milder south; a century or more to maturity in contrast to some sixty or seventy years. Southern timberlands can yield a harvest of pulpwood in the space of a generation. On cut-over land – or burnt-over land, for forest fires are a summer hazard – the birch and alder are the first colonisers. The birch adds lightness to the sombreness of the dark conifers. At higher altitudes and in higher latitudes it also forms a transitional zone between the thin pine stands and the open tundra with its lichens and shattered rocks.

Industrialists exploiting the manifold properties of

softwood timber neglected the birch; but countryfolk have always appreciated its value. Birch bark was peeled for lining roofs and for plaiting into shoes, satchels and boxes. Timbers were split for shingling. Birch twigs were bound together for besoms, kitchen and bathhouse whisks. In time of grain shortage, the cortex beneath the bark was pulverised and mixed with flour to eke out supplies. The birch also has an aesthetic appeal. In springtime, its mouse-ear leaves are encouraged to sprout when twigs are brought indoors for Easter decorations.

The woodlands at large touch other senses. As the foliage of the birch bursts forth over hundreds of thousands of hectares, heated by the sun by day and chastened by low temperatures at night, it yields a distinctive scent. Conifers, heated by summer sun, exude powerful, resinous odours. In the autumn the woodlands yield a pleasantly damp scent of decay. And woodland sounds are an essential part of the Swedish countryside – the summer breezes singing in the pines; the autumn gales roaring in the sprucewoods.

While the climax vegetation of Sweden may be coniferous forest, relatively little of today's timber cover is natural. Most of the woodlands that cover about half of Sweden consist of tree crops for harvesting. Proverbially, the forest was the mantle of the poor, providing building materials, fuel, and light in the shape of pine torches. Locally, considerable areas were subject to burn-beating or swidden cultivation, while summer grazing by animals was an additional destructive practice. Simultaneously, the seemingly inexhaustible resource was exploited for charcoal, pitch, tar and turpentine. And, before these activities declined, get-rich-quick, nineteenth-century timber barons clear-cut and destroyed widespread stands.

Today, Sweden's forests are jealously regulated through scientific management. Seeds are carefully selected from the best trees, seedlings are planted, fertilised, thinned and trimmed; land is drained, stands are rotationally cut. In fact, so thoroughly have the woodlands been changed by man that conservationists have had difficulty in finding samples of original timber stands to preserve for posterity. The residual *urskog* or primeval woodlands, with their stag-headed trees, dead, dying and decaying timbers festooned with hairy lichens, moss-covered and fungoid, have become protected wildernesses.

For many, the lesser vegetation of the forests means

more than the trees themselves. No child who has wandered in the summer sprucewoods will escape the stain of blueberries on fingers, lips and clothes. The housewife, plastic bucket in hand, finds more appeal in the dark-red lingon or whortleberry, the natural preservatives of which enable it to be kept throughout the winter and enjoyed as a relish with meat. Cranberry and cloudberry may be gathered from the boggier lands. In autumn, before they are touched by frosts, a score of different kinds of edible fungi (as well as a few poisonous ones) add colour to the woods and attract mushrooming expeditions.

As well as having an economic function, Swedish woodlands have had a spiritual role. In pagan times, supernatural qualities were ascribed to certain groves of trees. Indeed, with the coming of Christianity, mediaeval laws proscribed visits to such profane places. Woodlands have also been places of sanctuary. They have offered protection for those wishing to isolate themselves from society and for those wishing to escape the law. For more than one Swedish man of letters, the spruce woods are a part of the soul of his native land for which no olive grove, despite its sunnier setting, could ever compensate. It is in the woodlands that most of the ancestors of present-day Swedes pioneered their homesteads. Swedes remain very much men and women of the trees. The physical and mental refreshment of the present-day sport of orienteering springs from its forest setting. The autumn woods are the haunt of elk hunters. Nor is it surprising that wood as well as woodland should have inspired its own poetry –

Inside wood there ticks a clock
or perhaps a heart.
Wood is time,
Stratified like waves on a shore.

Artur Lundqvist's *Love of Wood* is an affection universally shared.

The forests of the southern third of Sweden are transitional between the coniferous forests of the north and the familiar oak and beechwoods of central Europe. Place names recall the formerly widespread distribution of oakwoods which were largely felled for shipbuilding – especially for naval vessels – and for constructional work.

Each type of countryside has its particular flora. In the springtime, the birch and spruce groves are first awakened by the blue *anemone hepatica*, which yields in turn to the white anemone, the lily-of-the-valley and the fragile pink flower, *linnea borealis*, which Linnaeus named after himself. The natural meadowlands offer the greatest diversity of flowers – including the protected fritillary. On the peatlands there are broad stretches of fluffy white bog cotton. In the high latitude fells, the crisp, grey reindeer moss yields to colourful lichens and a diminutive Alpine flora. The edges of the wasteland offer the wild strawberry and the wild raspberry. The lakes have their water lilies and water buttercups, with yellow irises around their margins and the tall rushes called *phragmites*, which serve a number of purposes for the farmer. Along the Baltic seaboard there are pioneering seashore plants. The island of Gotland boasts a distinctive blue flora, reproduced everywhere on tourist souvenirs – speedwell, pansy, forget-me-not, cornflower, chicory, vetch, *anemone pulsatila* and many others.

The woodlands remain the habitat of a range of wild animals – the fur-bearers – ermine, mink, fox (the two latter widely farmed), bear (still hunted a century ago, but now protected), wolverine and lynx and the occasional wolf. There are several kinds of deer. The imperturbable, loping elk is everywhere and is a major traffic hazard. An annual cull of some 100,000 is insufficient to keep numbers under control. The squirrel is ubiquitous, as much at home in the town as in the country and the lemming still swarms in the north. Birds – capercailzie, magpie, sparrow and a few others apart – are largely migratory: the seabirds (their skerry nesting grounds protected), the waders (crane, heron and the occasional stork), the swimmers (swans, geese and wild duck), the game birds, the swallows and swifts (thriving on clouds of midges and mosquitoes in the high north). Nor is the occasional eagle unknown.

The Character of the Farmsteads

Woodlands are complemented by trim farmlands which cover some seven per cent of the countryside. Most Swedish farmers – or *bönder*, as they call themselves – are owner-occupiers, and most are forest farmers, with the size of the forest holding increasing northwards. A small number of farmers combine fishing and farming. Animal husbandry dominates and ley farming is widespread, with silage production exceeding the hay harvest. Only in the remoter and more backward areas can the picturesque hay frames and harvest pikes be seen. Barley, oats and winter wheat lead among the cereals. Oil seed crops announce themselves with their vivid yellow flowers over the southern third of the country, while Skåne has sugar beet as a speciality. Yields of crops are about twice as high in the south as in the north of the country. Dairy products exceed domestic needs, and there have been restraints upon their production. Capital investment is high, not least because of the need to keep livestock, equipment and feeding stuffs under cover during the winter months. In the north, the outdoor grazing period may not be more than four or five months. Immense barns, sometimes three storeys high, characterise most farms. Tiled and clapboarded farmhouses, today built upon concrete basements, but formerly built upon a foundation of large boulders or granite blocks, are set in the informality of the kitchen garden's fruit trees and bushes. Roses, honeysuckle, phlox, peonies and tiger lilies crowd around the frequently covered porch or verandah. Yesterday's potato cellar and ice house often sit incongruously beside the tower of today's silo. Many farmhouses are still painted with the traditional Falun red – a preservative, near ox-blood in colour, which derives its name from the copper mine where it was first produced. Together with the less frequent yellow ochre and the occasional pastel washes, the colours add much to the attraction of the countryside.

Most Swedish farmsteads tend to be dispersed rather than nucleated in church villages. This is principally because of the land redistribution that occurred during the later eighteenth and early nineteenth centuries, when the open fields, with their scattered strips of cultivated land, were consolidated into unitary holdings. As in the other Nordic countries, farmers benefit from old-established agricultural cooperative organisations for wholesale purchasing (not least of equipment for the highly mechanised farming operations) as well as for marketing, processing, insurance and banking. Numbers employed in farming, with related forestry and fishing, only amount to about seven per cent of the Swedish work force, but productivity has never been higher.

The Urbanisation of Sweden

For two generations, most Swedes have lived and worked in towns, many of which, enjoying the amenities of woodland and water, are like the garden cities of other countries. About a third of Sweden's population of 8.4 millions live in and around the three biggest cities – Stockholm, Gothenburg and Malmö.

Stockholm, settled in the Middle Ages on a stockade island at the point where Lake Mälaren drains into the Baltic Sea, became Sweden's capital in 1436. Today, the 1.5 million inhabitants of its metropolitan area are spread over rather more than a score of islands. It is a city of bridges and waterfronts, with an intensive daily schedule of ferries to Finland and Åland, and a summer shuttle of steamers to its archipelago. It has a profile of Renaissance and contemporary spires and towers – one of the most distinctive being the neo-romantic 1920s city hall. Stockholm is generously provided with formal and informal parks, with residual pine, spruce and birch stands among four generations of apartment buildings. Metropolitan Stockholm, efficiently tied together with an underground railway system, has suburbs extending some twenty kilometres in all directions from its island core. 'Summer Stockholm' embraces thousands of leisure homes on thousands of islands on the seaward side of the city.

In contrast, Gothenburg, Sweden's largest port, on the breezy west coast and echoing with ships' sirens, extends along the tidal reaches of the deep Göta River. Dutch engineers helped its founders to construct canals as part of the seventeenth century system of fortifications. The Göta River is canalised for sea-going ships as far as Lake Vänern. Wharves and shipyards line its banks, and its estuary accommodates Scandinavia's largest container harbour. Some 250km south of Gothenburg is Sweden's third city, Malmö. It is an old Hanseatic settlement on the sandy shores of the Öresund, bound by a shuttle of ferries to Copenhagen, with fortress, administrative buildings and shipyards lying cheek by jowl.

South Sweden has a variety of coastal settlements. There are fishing ports such as Smögen and Fiskebäckskil amid the grey rocks of Bohuslän, which are taken over seasonally by summer yachts and holiday crowds. Bastad, Falsterbo and Ystad also offer idyllic holiday cottages and camping sites. There is Sweden's leading ferry port of Helsingborg, gateway to Denmark, which is not a little apprehensive about the possible construction of a bridge over the Öresund. There are exceptional settlements such as Karlskrona, a seventeenth century planned town which is Sweden's naval base and the haunt of inquisitive foreign submarines. Some tens of kilometres to the north is Kalmar, whose renaissance castle surveys a six-kilometre-long bridge which links the windmilled island of Öland to the mainland. Most memorable of all is the city of Visby on the island of Gotland. Here, some three kilometres of limestone walls enclose the remains of no fewer than sixteen churches and some attractive eighteenth century living quarters. It is a city of ruins and roses which seems to have been transported from the isles of Greece to this "northern Mediterranean".

The Bothnian coast of Sweden has a series of coastal towns with one common characteristic. All owe something of their livelihood to softwood timber processing, and almost all are situated on or near the estuary of a major river artery which opens up forested back country. Most were established in the seventeenth century and derived their original wealth from pitch, tar and ships' timbers. The monopoly of their trade was for some time held by the capital – hence Stockholm tar. Each has some distinguishing characteristic – be it the sheer size of softwood undertakings around Gävle and Sundsvall, the extensive university campus of Umeå, the state iron and steel plant of northerly Luleå, the picturesque, timber-built section of Örnsköldsvik, or the beautifully restored church precinct, with its converted stabling, at Lövänger.

Most of the towns of interior Sweden, a considerable number of which began as markets centred around a mediaeval church, have lacustrine or riverside settings. Representative of them are those distinguished by the suffix *köping* (which means a market) and which announce themselves all over the map of south Sweden – Falköping, Enköping, Jönköping, Lidköping, Norrköping, Nyköping. The concentration of metal-working settlements in the south-centre of Sweden known as Bergslagen is unique in Scandinavia. The oldest of the settlements dates from the Middle Ages. Most reached the peak of their importance during the 17th and 18th centuries, when Sweden was Europe's principal source of bar iron. They still remain a colourful group of communities. Some bear the names of the falls that provided their water power (Hällfors, Storfors, Degerfors): some, of their hammer ponds (Hallstahammar, Surahammar). Some have lost their original functions, and have become almost museum settlements, containing the remains of early factories and forges, echoing caves and tunnels of deserted mines, and the mansions of the ironmasters often set in landscaped estates. But the charcoal pits no longer smoke and the teams of horses, bearded with icicles, no longer sledge ore, fuel and bar iron over the winter snow. Towns such as Ludvika, Fagersta, Avesta and Sandvikon retain something of their original activity, though they look to electricity as their source of energy, and may even import raw materials.

In some respects, the most remarkable town in Bergslagen is Falun, site of Europe's oldest and, at one time, largest coppermine. The great hole in the ground, from the galleries of which ore was mined for some six hundred years, is rimmed with the reds, ochres and yellows of the weathered tailings. The nearby museum speaks of a long history of technical and mechanical ingenuity, while its sheets of copper money, some as big as roofing tiles, tell of the wealth that the mine once yielded.

The Bergslagen settlements look to the shores of Lake Mälaren, where Örebro used to gather together their products for shipment to the control point of the iron trade in Stockholm. Time was, as the Swedish novelist Hjalmar Bergman put it, when you "could feel Mother Svea's pulse" in Örebro on a market day. The pulse is more accurately assessed by the neighbouring city of Västerås today. Its electrical and electronic plants a consequence of past enterprise and present innovation, are the epitome of modern Swedish industry.

It will soon be a century since the centre of iron production in Sweden shifted away from the towns of Bergslagen to the fells of Lapland. Here, the phosphoric ores, the exploitation of which came with the discovery of the Gilchrist Thomas process of smelting in the 1870s, account for Sweden's largest raw material output. As much as 20 million tonnes a year are transported to the rail terminals of Narvik and Luleå for export. The town at the centre of the operations is Kiruna, commanding the outlines of the iron ranges of Kirunavaara and Luossavaara and, more distantly, Kebnekaise, Sweden's loftiest mountain. Kiruna is located well within the Arctic Circle and, despite its sensitivity to world ore prices, has probably been the most successful of the world's high latitude mining communities. Kiruna is also one of the exceptions that prove the rule about Swedish towns being born of water.

There are others, but none more distinguished than the university cities of Uppsala and Lund. Uppsala, site of Sweden's archbishopric and of Scandinavia's oldest university, commanding the rich plains of the province of Uppland, is set beside the small river Fyris, today of little more than aesthetic consequence. From the Gothic-spired cathedral and the bulky, eighteenth-century castle, it is only several kilometres as the crow flies to the group of massive tumuli that identify Gamla (or old) Uppsala. Lund, whose university precinct is assembled round Scandinavia's most substantial Romanesque cathedral, has a Central European appearance. It is set in one of Sweden's most extensive arable areas, cultivated for centuries by the plough – and it has managed to succeed in life without any significant presence of rocks, water or coniferous forest.

Because it was the cheapest and most available material, most Swedish towns were formerly constructed of wood; stone being reserved for ecclesiastical, military and administrative buildings. Not surprisingly, fire has been a constant hazard. In the seventeenth century, reconstruction following a conflagration was already subject to a number of controls. Most commonly, a grid-iron pattern of streets and open spaces was imposed, with official buildings and residences on building plots of regulated size. Many Swedish towns still display the geometrical and somewhat repetitive results of this early planning legislation.

In Sweden, as in most of Scandinavia, a considerable number of settlements have grown up around a single factory or mine, at the same time serving a farming area. They are most common in Sweden's so-called 'forest communes'. Not infrequently they develop into problem settlements as the resource that gave rise to them is exhausted or changes its market value. Since they are usually distant from the main centres of population, they do not benefit from the 'green wave' that has been affecting Swedish cities over the last generation, with migration from the built-up areas beyond the suburbs to the rural retreat which the Americans call exurbia.

The Leisure Home

Given the spaciousness of Sweden and its low population density, its citizens have the possibility of spreading themselves. In winter, however, there is something to be said for huddling together.

During the brief summer, with its long, bright days, there is a widespread urge to escape from the town. As a result, Sweden has fully 300,000 leisure homes and their number is multiplying fast. A leisure home may be a large, gently decaying villa, ornate with fretwork, follies and verandahs – fit setting for a nostalgic, Ingmar Bergman film – or a sleek, modern, pre-fabricated structure. It may be a restored, formerly abandoned farmhouse, or a modest shack which just about reaches planning requirements. Many farmers build summer residences for let. Again, a waterside setting is favoured,

with the result that legislative controls on development have become increasingly strict. Concentrations of summer residences, without adequate water supply and sewage facilities, threaten to pollute lakes and rivers.

After the physical restraints of winter, the summer residence offers compensating liberty. Dress is minimal. Shoes are cast off, not least for the pleasure of feeling the different kinds of vegetation and soil under the soles of the feet. The fishing rod is fetched out, and the nets are set. Luck may bring a salmon, or at least a lavaret. Pike are trapped, and crayfish are sought for August parties. Such a life is a retreat into the past. Children live the life of their ancestors in the forest. For adults there seems to be an almost masochistic urge to reject temporarily the material comforts of urban existence, and to adopt a slower pace of life. At the same time, a leisure home, which is available to most families, implies mobility. Many such homes would be largely inaccessible without Sweden's three million automobiles and the hundreds of thousands of leisure boats. They would also be less desirable were not the cocoon of security in respect of health services so readily available.

Leisure homes may be winterised, especially those in the solitudes of the interior and the northern uplands. Here, they also meet the needs of autumn hunters and winter skiers. But, again, accessibility for motor transport is essential. Snow plough and snow blower keep open highway, byway, and runway. The snowmobile operates on winter routes, and even the Lapp has his skidoo.

Problems of the Northland

The affluence that these facilities suggest is widespread, but not universal. Sweden has an uneven distribution of population, of resources, of investment and of income and, generally speaking, it is the northern third – perhaps even half – of the country that suffers on most scores. The situation is inseparable from what has been called the discipline of distance. Sweden at large is distant from the markets of western Europe: northern Sweden suffers the consequences of even greater remoteness. Above all, distance results in higher transport costs both for exports and imports. At the same time, living costs are greater in the north than in the south principally because of the climatic circumstances. Snow may lie on the ground for six months, temperatures may remain below zero for weeks on end, and ice may close some of the Bothnian ports. The costs of heating, of building, of clothing and of vehicle maintenance that are imposed by the longer duration of winter levy additional taxes on the individual, the community and the manufacturing enterprise.

Given the Swedish policy of social and economic security, it is natural that attempts are made to compensate for the remoteness and the climatic circumstances of the north land. For this purpose, Sweden is divided into a number of support regions, with assistance and subsidisation calculated according to the degree of hardship in each. Thus, rail transport is subsidised in order to harmonise the purchase and sale prices of many commodities between the south and the north. Long distance telephone calls to and from the north have special rates. Employees in government service, who constitute over a third of the total Swedish labour force, and who may account for the majority of those employed in some Norrland communities, are compensated for some of the extra costs encountered in daily living. Again, northern Sweden suffers more than the south from seasonal unemployment and underemployment. As a result, efforts have been made to promote manufacturing activity. An outstanding example is provided by investment in a state-owned iron and steel plant at the port of Luleå and the assistance given to a group of associated metallurgical industries. The education industry has also helped development. The university at Umeå probably accounts for the employment of about a quarter of the total population of the city. Tourism assists, but the summer season is short and employment opportunities are in any case best at the time when holiday traffic reaches its peak. Winter sports bring only a limited income to the high fells in February and March.

It is understandable that people should tend to move away from the underprivileged to seemingly more privileged areas. The drift from the countryside to the towns, long past in the south, continues in north Sweden. There is also a migration from the towns of the north to those of the south, though its effect on population numbers in the north is partly offset by the fact that the birth-rate remains higher in the north. However, over extensive areas of Norrland, population migration is such that many communities are experiencing noticeable farm and land abandonment, and an increase in the proportion of elderly and retired citizenry as a result of the movement of the younger and more enterprising elements.

Such a situation adds to the difficulties of local administration and provision of amenities. Today, it is estimated that the minimum number of inhabitants required to support a school complex, an old people's home, a medical centre, a post office, appropriate banks and stores is about 8-9,000. The difficulties are exaggerated when the population is scattered. Mobile services, from stores and libraries to dental and medical clinics, may achieve economies, but the social fabric suffers when these institutions no longer have fixed premises.

The people of Norrland in general, and of Norrbotten in particular, have evolved their own attitudes to the south. 'Sweden lay far away and was in fact another land', wrote the Norrbotten author Eyvind Johnson as he recalled his youth in the early twentieth century. The northerners cannot be independent of the south, and they resent what they regard as exploitation of their resources by southern industrialists and administrators. Resentment is expressed in radical attitudes and a relatively high communist vote. At the same time, religious circles are characterised by a strong pietist element which contrasts with the relaxed evangelical Lutheran spirit that prevails over most of the country.

The north country has another distinguishing feature. Jointly with adjacent parts of Norway and Finland, it is a territory of ethnographic diversity. The Lapps, who were the original inhabitants of north Sweden, number some 15,000, but in all respects make a disproportionate impact. Most of the *Samer*, as they call themselves, are permanently settled on farm holdings, but a minority continues to pursue the traditional way of life in reindeer husbandry. Their colourful costumes may suggest that they are a quaint relic from the past, but they have an increasingly strong ethnic sense and have acquired a political voice. In Jokkmokk, they have their own cultural centre, with a high school and museum. Their herds of some 275,000 reindeer may add to the *fantasia arctica*, but they have to be viewed practically as well as romantically. The annual slaughter provides a substantial income in the shape of processed meat, skins and horn. At the same time, the problem of grazing capacity, leading to trespass, makes for continuous friction between reindeer owner, farmer and forester. Contrastingly, the development of Norrbotten through rail, road and hydro-electric power installations has been at the expense of traditional grazing lands and migration routes.

North Sweden faces a second ethnographic issue. The border lands with Finland along the Torne valley have always had a substantial Finnish-speaking population. The opening up of forestry in north Sweden and of iron mining in Norrbotten attracted considerable numbers of immigrant Finns. With the establishment of a common labour market between the countries of Norden, the inflow of Finns increased. At one time, in the mid 1970s, Sweden had some 300,000 Finns resident within its borders, the largest of its many minority groups. As with the Lapps, the Finns have sought minority rights, especially in their use of Finnish for educational purposes.

Sweden's north country remains very much frontier land. It is an extensive, thinly peopled, almost semi-colonial territory of primary production. It is a kind of Jack London country, a land of adventure – and often of adventures. The Prospectors, surveyors and engineers are there; Conservationists are there keeping an eye on them; and exploration societies revel in it. The frontier of settlement ebbs and flows across it in response to the changing values of its resourses. Nor can it be forgotten that the province of Norrbotten is frontier country in a political sense. Today, movement across its boundary rivers is unrestricted – a network of marriages links Swedish and Finnish families on either bank. Nevertheless, the whole of north-eastern Norrbotten contains extensive closed military areas. Before the First World War, a major military outpost was established at Boden: during the Second World War, the north was under the threat of invasion.

Sweden balances the past and the future in its north country. Visually, it displays much that recalls the Sweden of yesterday: resource-wise it is difficult to deny that it is a territory with a future. Yet the future is unpredictable because of the changing nature of Sweden's wealth-producing activities. Paradoxically, they depend less upon indigenous raw materials than they did a generation – let alone two generations – ago. Ironically, the primary producing inhabitants of the north country are heavily supported by the service sector of the economy, for contemporary Sweden derives much from the services as well as the goods that it sells to the world.

The Technological Transformation

Sweden was late in undergoing its industrial revolution, partly because it lacked coal at a time when coal was the principal industrial fuel. It was also a country somewhat reluctant to import foreign capital upon which to build new enterprises. Contrastingly, it bred a remarkable company of inventors who contributed to the country's industrial emergence, and who left their mark on the world.

The inventors included Gustaf de Laval, who produced the original cream separator and early versions of the milking machine, and Alfred Nobel, inventor of the dynamite that was critical for mining and constructional operations in the hard rocks of Sweden. L.M. Ericsson produced the telephone in Sweden at about the same time as Alexander Bell did so in Canada; Husqvarna conceived a sewing machine to rival Singer; S.K.F. inventors perfected the vital ball-bearing industry and Dalén invented automatic lighthouses (a boon to the Nordic countries with their extended and hazardous coasts). Sweden had an almost world-wide match monopoly before the crash of the Kreuger empire in the 1930s. Innovative improvements have been no less important, especially in the field of long-distance electrical transmission. It is difficult to explain this concentration of activity. The Swedish aphorism that poverty encourages ingenuity – usually referring specifically to the province of Småland – hardly applies to the inventors themselves. Sweden's early adoption of the German model of higher technical education may have played a part; but education alone cannot account for the fact that Sweden is one of the three leading countries in the world in the number of patents registered annually.

In no field has development been more striking than in transport. Swedish State Railways were among the first in Europe to be completely electrified, and Sweden was one of the first countries to have a national electricity grid. It was natural that the production of rolling stock, of an electrical components industry and of electro-metallurgy should follow. But the impressive development of the automobile industry is less easy to explain. Within the span of a generation, Sweden has captured a world market in heavy goods vehicles and buses, as well as in passenger cars. As an extension of the automobile industry, Sweden also entered the field of aircraft production, though for military rather than civil reasons. Meanwhile, marine transport claimed equal attention for, as with the other Nordic countries, sea-going is a traditional part of Swedish life. The expertise gained in the many small shipyards that built the fishing craft and wooden-hulled, cooperatively-owned sailing ships contributed much to the rise of a modern ship-building industry: so, too, did the production of specialised steels. Large-scale shipbuilding was concentrated on the west coast, especially at Gothenburg, Malmö and Uddevalla. For a brief period, Swedish shipbuilding claimed world attention, especially in respect of its labour relations; but it has suffered from the decline in world trade following the oil crisis. Uddevalla's yards are closed, and Malmö's have largely ceased operation.

Of all Swedish industries, those based upon timber are most widely distributed. They announce themselves throughout the country by their waterside locations, their tall chimneys with plumes of white smoke, and the powerful odour emitted by the sulphite process. Generally speaking, softwood plants are major complexes yielding a variety of products. Paper and pulp, deals and wallboards are simply raw materials for an ever-increasing range of goods. Nor can by-producers be ignored. Chemicals above all constitute a major branch of Swedish industry.

Design and quality in consumer goods were clearly evident in the inter-war years. Glass was brought to the attention of the world through success at international exhibitions. A particular Swedish style, variant upon Scandinavian themes, emerged in household products, from furniture, through textiles, ceramics, cutlery and tableware to kitchen products. Clothing followed, the Swedes having pioneered leatherwear in response to their winter needs and as a result of the abundance of elk and reindeer skins. And the word *smörgåsbord* came in with the household goods, introducing the range of Swedish delicatessen and crispbreads that characterises the cold table.

The Swedish market is relatively small, and the economies of scale in industry can only be achieved by exporting. Some major firms, such as the telephone systems company Ericsson, export well over 90 per cent of their products. Other firms have diversified their activities to spread their sales more widely. Thus, the hydraulics firm of Atlas Copco lists 3,000 different products and services. At the same time as Swedish industry has expanded and diversified at home, it has established daughter plants abroad. Most major Swedish industries now have a world-wide distribution of branches, especially those in the field of engineering and electronics. Banking, insurance and consultancy firms have similarly established overseas offices. As a result, the number of Swedes resident in some foreign cities is as large as the population of some of Sweden's home towns. The profits derived from their overseas plants by a number of leading Swedish companies exceeds those from the home plant. Sweden has also been highly successful in selling, assembling and providing operational instruction for entire production units. They range from paper and pulp plants to hydro-electric power stations, from mineral refining units to telephone systems, from bridges and airfields to educational institutions and hospitals. In the neighbourhood of Moscow, Swedes have constructed the world's largest dairy.

As a result of all this enterprise, it is not surprising that Sweden's per capita income is among the highest in the world. Given this solid economic foundation, it has also been able to establish and maintain one of the world's most complete systems of social security. But maintenance of the standards of achievement causes growing concern, not least because of the problem of energy.

Time was when Sweden rejoiced in abundant, cheap energy from its water power. But, in the inter-war years, demand was already growing to the extent that future shortages were anticipated, and water power rights across the Norwegian border were negotiated by the city of Stockholm. Today, most of Sweden's hydro-electric resources have been harnessed, and those that remain untapped are the cause of controversy between conservationists and developers. In the post-war years, Sweden became heavily dependent upon cheap imported Middle East oil, with half of its merchant fleet consisting of tankers. Unlike Norway, it lacks domestic oil resources, with only a little oil shale and possible prospects of limited supplies off its coast. The problem of energy deficiency is heightened because of the widespread opposition to nuclear power. Sweden has twelve reactors, but, following a referendum, it has been agreed to phase them out by 2010 A.D. Despite active programmes to conserve energy, it is evident that the Swedish economy will continue to be strained by the relatively high price of fuel.

National Romanticism

At the same time as Sweden has advanced economically and experimented socially, it has become increasingly interested in its past – a past full of contrasting experiences. In Sweden's present-day landscape there is an abundant legacy from earlier times, though it is less concentrated than in more populous lands. Earliest among the features are the Stone Age rock drawings – of boats, hunters, animalistic prey, spirals and labyrinths. There are familiar tumuli, and unfamiliar ship-shaped burial sites outlined by boulders. There are hundreds of rune stones, memorials erected to Varangians – or Vikings – who, for the most part journeyed east rather than west. Their adventures are racily fictionalised by Frans G. Bengtsson in his novel *Long Ships*. From the very names on signposts it is possible to piece together the story of the occupation and development of the land, for the scientific study of place names was pioneered by a Swedish philologist. South Sweden is rich in mediaeval churches, some of them partly fortified, some with finely restored wall paintings. It is also sprinkled with the ruins of religious houses, some founded in the name of Sweden's special saint, Birgitta. To the Middle Ages also belong the hoards of gold and silver coins, stamped with the heads of Old World monarchs, emperors and caliphs who ruled before the Swedish state existed, which have been recovered from Gotland.

After the Reformation, Sweden rose to become a European power, with complete control over the Baltic Sea. In the seventeenth century, it was the leader of Protestant armies on the continent, its king Gustavus II rejoicing in the title 'The lion of the north'. Formidable castles, such as Gripsholm on the peaceful waters of Lake Mälaren or Baroque Kalmar and pleasure palaces such as Läckö, recall the age of greatness. Loot from the Thirty Years War, glass-cased in Stockholm, sparkles as in an Aladdin's cave. The ill-fated warship *Vasa*, which turned turtle on putting to sea some three hundred years ago, has been lifted from the water and is displayed in all its glory. Even after the defeat at Poltava by the Russians of the adventurous Charles XII, hero of a history by Voltaire, Sweden retained a leading, though different, position in Europe. The Age of Enlightenment witnessed the establishment of an Academy of Sciences graced by men of such genius as Linnaeus, Celsius and Polhem, who was sometimes called the da Vinci of the north. The military organisation of the seventeenth century yielded to a spirit of scientific enquiry. Among other initiatives, Sweden set in motion the world's first modern census in 1750. And, while Gustavus III brought cultural life to a high peak at the summer palace of Drottningholm (Sweden's counterpart to Versailles), the taverns of Stockholm echoed with the songs of Bellman, a latter-day troubadour whose airs are familiar throughout Sweden to this day.

Between the monuments from Sweden's past and the comfortable living quarters of the present, the poverty and privation of much of nineteenth century Sweden, when the country became a poor relation in the family of European nations, tends to be overlooked. The shacks of the landless rural proletariat, and the rough barracks built to accommodate migrant industrial workers beside the money-making timber mills, have disappeared. But the lot of Sweden's poor was the spur to Vilhelm Moberg's epic work, *The Emigrants*, which epitomises the experiences of a full million Swedes who sought a new life in the New World. Ironically, two of the provinces that contributed most abundantly to the stream of emigrants, Värmland (home of the creator of Nils Holgersson) and the 'wooden shoe country' of Småland, have become two of the most appealing tourist areas, while rocky Bohuslän, described in the nineteenth century as 'one great poorhouse', is a summer holiday haven.

An appraisal of Sweden's past, warts and all, owes much to its museums. While August Strindberg was reinterpreting the succession of Swedish monarchs through his historical dramas, Arthur Hazelius was conceiving a new kind of museum at the grass roots level. Skansen, as his creation was called, was located on one of the inner islands of Stockholm, Djurjarden. It was founded in 1891 as the first of a new type of open air museum. To it were brought representative dwellings and workshops of different ages and localities. They were furnished, equipped and decorated in the style of their periods, and brought to life by craftsmen taking to their forges, mills, workbenches or glass moulds, with womenfolk (rather less self-conscious than the men in their folk dress) taking to their spinning wheels, looms or the making of lace pillows. Skansen has been copied in all parts of Sweden, independently of the establishment of a range of museums specific to particular enterprises or pursuits – the match museum at Jönköping, the House of the Emigrants at Växjö, the forestry museum at Sundsvall, the silver mining museum in remote Arjeplog.

The endowments of some areas have made them virtual folk museums in their own right. Lake Siljan and its inhabitants were already immortalised in the vivid canvases of Anders Zorn a century ago; but it was not long before picturesque hotels were built for Swedes who wished to visit his territory. The local arts and crafts also exerted an attraction – clocks with their richly painted cases, wood-carvings (above all the blue, red and orange Dalarna horses) and weaving, all bearing distinctive decorative motifs. The pinkish-grey limestone, rich in fossils, was to be admired in polished floors, around lintels and on tombstones. Churchyards also contained memorials which testified to the blacksmith's art as well as to the deceased who were identified by profession as well as by name, as are their descendants in contemporary telephone catalogues.

In summer the churchboat, with its team of costumed rowers, still plies the lake at Leksand or Rättvik; the decorated midsummer pole is still raised; fiddle and concertina still play for folk dances. Nor is winter without a climax. On the first Sunday in March, thousands of skiers assemble in Mora to repeat the epic run (or at least part of it) made by King Gustavus Vasa rather more than four hundred years ago.

There are other ceremonies which recall the past. Some surround the monarchy, with coaches, horses and mounted guards being fetched out as occasion demands. In the vaulted cellars of Stockholm castle, there is a theatrical display of royal costumes and mementoes – and a coffee room where special cakes are eaten on the November day that commemorates the seventeenth century hero King Gustavus Adolphus. A more cheerful celebration (though the weather may be bleak) is the rite of spring enjoyed by students on Walpurgis Eve, the night before the public holiday of May 1st. More formal university ceremonies call for white ties and tail suits – with top hats for the women, as well as the men, who hold doctor's degrees. The grandest ceremony of all is reserved for the annual Nobel Prize gathering.

A Concern for Conservation

Commemoration of the past is accompanied by a concern for the conservation of nature. In some areas this has deep roots. In the eighteenth century, Swedish administrators were disturbed at the inroads being made upon the woodlands, and sought to restrain destructive practices such as burning-over the land for crop cultivation. Conservation of areas of outstanding scenic value was initiated before the First World War, not least through the influence of the well-established Swedish Tourist Board. Six of Sweden's nineteen national parks were in being by 1909, including two in the northern highlands which remain among the largest in Europe. Today, there are more than a thousand nature reserves. They range from distinctive peatland habitats to representative hazel and oak groves along the Baltic shore (some of which Linnaeus regarded as finer than noblemen's parks). There are also some 450 wildlife protection areas, not least the numerous breeding grounds of seabirds in the skerries. In order to control the development of coastal areas, the Swedish littoral has been divided into three types of zone – those which are already industrialised and where additional manufacturing plants may be located; those where industrial development is prohibited, and those areas where the economic and social needs of the inhabitants are sufficiently pressing for industrial development to take precedence over conservation.

Pollutants cause much concern. Sensitivity is registered by the introductory tables of Sweden's statistical yearbook, with their lists of chemicals and pesticides applied by type and area, the degree of emission of pollutants in particular cities, and the distribution of oil spillages. Swedish forests and lakes are also seriously affected by acid rain, which probably derives in equal quantities from east and west European sources. Sweden aims to reduce its own sulphur emissions by the installation of improved, Swedish-designed equipment at all of its thermal power stations (stations which will increase in number in the future) and to reduce automobile fumes. As for nuclear energy, uranium may no longer be mined in Sweden, while the export of reactors and reactor technology has been discontinued.

While pollution of Sweden's lakes and rivers can be constrained by legislation, pollution of the international waters of the Baltic Sea is only subject to nominal control. As a non-tidal, inland sea of low salinity with some of its shores heavily industrialised, the Baltic could easily become northern Europe's dead sea. Sweden plays a leading role in supporting the permanent international research body that monitors its waters.

The Search for Security

Life in Sweden has been, and remains, a continuing search for security – security in three areas. First, there has been the pursuit of security of life and limb. A century ago, much of rural Sweden was still afflicted by the threat of famine, while the expanding cities were acquiring an industrial proletariat, many of whom lived in poverty. Technological developments have replaced poverty with affluence; deficiency with surfeit. The hazards of living on the northern frontiers of settlement in Europe – let alone within the confines of the Arctic Circle – can never be eliminated; but they can be offset. Health and welfare legislation have guaranteed personal security, and to a large extent evened out the disparities that exist between those who work in different parts of the country. It is doubtful if the benefits derived from the social security programme are surpassed anywhere in the world.

In the second place, there has been a steadily expanding mixed economy on which social security reposes. Policy has been directed towards a middle way between state-led and privately operated industry in which employee participation is a distinguishing feature.

Thirdly, there has been a concern for international security and this has been sought by adopting a policy of neutrality in world affairs. Sweden has not been involved in a war since 1808-9, when it lost the Grand Duchy of Finland to imperial Russia. Its frontier with Norway, eventually mapped along the mountainous divide in the 1750s, has proved one of the two most stable in Europe. It has no overseas possessions, the colonies on the Delaware having been absorbed by the British at the end of the seventeenth century. It has no territorial ambitions, nor has it agitated for an extension of its territorial waters. It seeks to maintain northern Europe as a low tension area in international politics.

Nevertheless, its neutrality is well-armed. No trumpets and drums announce the fact the Sweden has a defensive air force second to none in Europe and that it can call upon a large reserve army based upon male conscription. The name Bofors alone suggests an efficient and effective back-up of armaments. Superficially, there is no evidence of strong national feeling in Sweden, yet the blue-and-gold flag stands for an independent and determined spirit.

Her Nordic neighbours are important to Sweden, and Swedish security is strongest when they are most harmonious. Although it is a small power in an international context, Sweden is the largest of the five Nordic countries. The five are more closely integrated into a community than any other group of sovereign states in the world. Out of the deliberations of the Nordic Council, which was established in 1952, has sprung much common legislation which has been to the advantage of all. Perhaps most important is the fact that the five countries constitute a common passport area and a common labour market. As the wealthiest and most centrally located, Sweden has tended to receive the maximum number of immigrants from its neighbours. Indeed, thanks to a generous immigration policy, about one in ten Swedes is either an immigrant or has been born of immigrant parents.

Through its neutral stance, Sweden is able to maintain an independent line among neighbours who have different allegiances. To the west, Norway, Denmark and Iceland belong to N.A.T.O. To the east, Finland has a Treaty of Friendship and Understanding with the U.S.S.R. All five are members of E.F.T.A., which had its origin in Stockholm a generation ago; but Denmark is a member of the E.E.C. and Finland has a special relationship with Comecon.

Today, there is a fourth dimension to Sweden's search for security – the economic and social security of others. Sweden devotes a greater proportion of its gross national product to helping the insecure and improverished parts of the world than almost any other country. What is more, its contributions to international aid and to the maintenance of international order are the more acceptable because of its neutrality in the political arena and its independent attitudes to world power groupings.

In the final place, there can only be degrees of security, and all attempts to reduce old hazards and uncertainties will be accompanied by new risks. Since the days of Nils Holgersson, Swedes have triumphed over the limitations of their natural environment by the rational application of technical facilities, and they have established one of the highest standards of living in the world by striking an effective if controversial balance between the public and private sectors of the economy. If Swedes have not found the formula for guaranteeing the greatest happiness of the greatest number, they have taken at least one step in the right direction by discovering the circumstances that make for the greatest longevity of the greatest number. And most outside observers would agree that, given the size, setting and population of their country, they have come as near to creating a model social and economic system as is likely to be possible.

Sweden grew up as a nation at the meeting ground of Lake Mälaren and the Baltic Sea. The core of the original Stockholm (right), dominated by Riddarholmen Church, contrasts with a view (above) looking east from Stadshuset (the City Hall). An hour's journey north of Stockholm is Uppsala, with its fine Gothic cathedral (previous page), the Lutheran archbishopric and Scandinavia's oldest university.

Previous pages: Stockholm, city of contrasts; (left) Riddarholmen and Stadshuset at sunset, and (right) Sergels torg with the tallest glass statue in the world (37,5 metres), the light column "Kristall". This page: changing the guard at the royal palace (below), (bottom) children at Stortorget in the Old Town, (right) sightseeing boats on Riddarfjärden. Opposite: Västerlånggatan, one of the exciting shopping streets in the Old Town.

Östergötland and Småland provinces in south-east Sweden flank Lake Vättern (above), Sweden's second largest lake. Right: Gränna, an attractive town in Småland, where Brahegatan offers a typical summer scene, with Swedish flags much in evidence. Overleaf: panoramic views of the lakeshore farmsteads from Brahe Hus castle, which dominates one of the many rocky outcrops; and of harbour lights at Gränna.

Kalmar, an historic town in the province of Småland in south-east Sweden, is centred on its sturdy castle (above) which commands the sound between the mainland and the island of Öland. In the centre of Kalmar, on Stortorget, is the baroque cathedral (left) typical of church architecture from the 17th-century, and contrasting strikingly with the Gothic features of Uppsala Cathedral.

The dry, open, limestone landscapes of the island of Öland throw into relief (top left) Gettlinge Gravfält, near Degerhamn – an iron-age stone circle – the ruins of Borgholm Castle (left), and the late 18th century Karls Olsgården house (above) at Himmelsberga open air museum. Top: the remarkable standing-stone circle at Kåseberga in the province of Skåne. Facing page: historic Visby (left), principal city of the island of Gotland (top right), is linked to the mainland by regular ferry services, while the 4-mile-long Öland Bridge (bottom right) carries traffic between Öland and the mainland.

Skåne, Sweden's southernmost province, was a part of Denmark until the 17th century. It is rich in historical monuments. Glimmingehus Castle, near Valby (right) is typical of the early fortified residences. The mediaeval church at Hagleholm (above) resembles many in Denmark. Skåne, sometimes called "the granary of Sweden" has extensive arable lands as illustrated (previous pages) by Abbekås (right) and Anderslöv (left), with its representative field of sugar beet.

The history of Malmö, third city of Sweden, is recalled in its museum (top left), St Peter's Church (top), carefully preserved old neighbourhoods (left) and leafy parkland (above). Stortorget (opposite) is at the centre. Malmö is on the Öresund with (overleaf) shipyards and lively boat links with Copenhagen (left), and a major railway terminus (right).

Västergötland, in west central Sweden, has the splendid Renaissance castle of Läckö (right and left). Nearby is the old settlement of Ulricehamn, with tourist huts (bottom left) and Ullsundet (bottom), an inlet of Sweden's largest lake, Vänern. Below: a typical Västergötland windmill.

Gothenburg, on the west coast, is Sweden's second city and principal container port. The port and shipbuilding yards are concentrated along the estuary of the Göta river. Left: four scenes viewed from the extensive port area. Opposite: some of the thousands of yachts that crowd the harbour.

Above: Gothenburg's canals, relics of an earlier fortification system, today carry tourist traffic. Left: Norra Hamngatan's stately classical buildings contrast with the central station (above). Korsgatan (opposite) is part of the shopping precinct. Overleaf: tramways are still maintained in Norrköping, Östergötland, (left) and the 17th century Kronhus (right) is put to new use.

Gothenburg is very much a cultural centre, with attractive parks (below), bridges (right), statuary such as Carl Milles' *Poseidon* (bottom right), art galleries and theatres. In the city centre are the Trädgårdsföreningen (opposite) and the handsome Gustav Adolfs torg (overleaf, left). The Maritime Museum (bottom) also has museum ships (overleaf, right).

Exposed Kungshamn Harbour, Bohuslän (opposite) contrasts with sheltered Langöberget (top) near Fjällbacka. Södra Dalsland province has the fine old Bolstad church (left) and Trollhättan locks (above) which bypass Trollhättan Falls (overleaf, left). Carlsten's castle, Marstrand (overleaf, right) guards the approach to Gothenburg.

Seasonal contrasts in Värmland. Winter scenes from Skutberget near Karlstad, with cross-country skiing and (top right) Lake Vänern's snow-clad shores. Overleaf: the old stone bridge at Karlstad (left), and Rottneros Hall (right), an aristocratic manor from the classical period.

Värmland, province of ironmasters and timbermen, settles down to winter. Left: late afternoon in Borgeby, near Sunne. Below: the restaurant at Skutberget. Bottom left: a country home at Skutberget. Bottom: beside Lake Valsjön, in neighbouring Dalarna. Right: a home in Brågstorp. Overleaf: snow-covered pine and spruce woods near Karlstad.

Lake Siljan, in the province of Dalarna, is central to one of the most attractive parts of Sweden. The Swedish Tourist Authority already sensed this at the turn of the century, while artists were not slow to establish their colonies around its shores. Midsummer, with picnics and folk dancing amid the lush limestone flora, is the climax of the year. Sunday morning churchgoers (left and far right) take to long church boats decorated with birch twigs and make their way to Rättvik church (bottom right). National costumes are fetched out for the occasion, while fiddlers accompany the proceedings. Overleaf, left: dusk after a storm on Lake Siljan, seen from Vidablick Tower at Rättvik. Overleaf right: the castle at Örebro, a market and manufacturing town in Närke province, central Sweden.

The province of Jämtland, in north central Sweden, lies adjacent to Norway, and its forested country (bottom right) is thinly peopled. Below: skiers come back to their cabins (right). In midwinter, days are short; (opposite) the blue twilight of the late afternoon gives a theatrical appearance to the church at Åre.

A century ago, winter was the season when man and beast stayed indoors to conserve energy. Today man has learned to appreciate all that a winter landscape offers. Åreskutan, above Åre in Jämtland (these pages) is a favourite winter playground. Overleaf, left: the scene around Åreskutan summit café.

Above: skiers in Åreskutan, their equipment reminding us that Scandinavia is the home of the ski. Top right and opposite: hang-gliding is a new sport to find its way into Åre, the ski slopes of which provide a backdrop.

Severe winters in the fields of Jämtland create ice fantasies out of waterfalls such as Tännforsen (left) near Åre. Below: a typical, red-painted farmhouse and (right) wooden barn near Sveg, with tractor and sled tracks from timber haulage. Bottom left: the cosy interior of Handöls Lapp chapel. Bottom right: the 19th century white wooden church at Duved.

Southern Lappland embraces extensive high fields along the Norwegian border. Jokkmokk, with its river (opposite) and Lapp museum (below and bottom right), is a focal point. The horse-drawn sled (right) is a familiar sight. So, too, are plain-faced churches such as that of Risbäck (bottom). Overleaf: southern Lappland's contrasting vistas: the bogland tundra of Stekenjokk (left) and the birch scrub of Vilhelmina.

The simplicity of the Lapp church at Jokkmokk (pictures left) contrasts, both inside and out, with the ornate confection of the main Lutheran church (below, bottom and opposite). Overleaf: southern Lappland's Kultsjön is rapids all the way on midsummer night (left) and midsummer day (right).